D1569381

Jam Session

Tara Lipinski

Terri Dougherty
ABDO Publishing Company

visit us at
www.abdopub.com

Published by ABDO Publishing Company, 4940 Viking Drive, Suite 622, Edina, Minnesota 55435.

Printed in the United States.

Cover and Interior Photo credits: AP/Wide World Photos

Edited by Denis Dougherty

Sources: Detroit Free Press; Knight-Ridder News; People Magazine; Sports Illustrated;
Sports Illustrated For Kids; USA Today

Library of Congress Cataloging-in-Publication Data

Dougherty, Terri.
   Tara Lipinski / Terri Dougherty.
        p.   cm. -- (Jam Session)
   Includes index.
   Summary: Discusses the personal life and skating career of the young woman who won a gold
medal in figure skating at the 1998 Olympics in Nagano, Japan.
   ISBN 1-57765-312-2 (hardcover)
   ISBN 1-57765-344-0 (paperback)
   1. Lipinski, Tara, 1982- --Juvenile literature.   2. Skaters--United States--Biography--Juvenile
literature. [1. Lipinski, Tara, 1982- . 2. Ice skaters. 3. Women--Biography.] I. Title. II.
Series.
   GV850.L56D68   1999
   796.91'2'092--dc21
   [b]   98-21920
                                               CIP
                                             AC

Contents

Striking Gold

A few hours before Tara Lipinski had a chance to realize her dream, she admitted something to her mom.

"I'm scared," the 15-year-old said.

Her mom was surprised. Tara never seemed afraid of anything. She had confidently won medals in figure skating contests all over the world. Now she had a chance to win a gold medal in the 1998 Winter Olympics.

Tara, after winning the women's free skating long program, kisses the gold.

Tara's mom knew the Olympics were special to her daughter. When she was only two years old, Tara pretended to win an Olympic medal. She stood on top of a plastic dish and imagined it was a medal stand. Then she took some ribbon and flowers and held her own medal ceremony.

Now she had a chance to win a medal for real.

"It's OK to be scared," Tara's mom, Pat Lipinski, told her. "It's good to be scared. But you can do it."

Later, Tara left for the White Ring arena in Nagano, Japan. But after she closed the door to her parents' room, she knocked lightly and leaned back in.

"I'm gonna do it," she said confidently.

Tara was right. She skated perfectly and had fun on the ice. She didn't just jump, she soared. She not only spun, she whirled. She nailed difficult combination jumps. After her performance, she ran across the ice with her arms raised.

As her marks were flashed across the board, she shrieked with excitement. She was the gold medal winner!

That night, Tara slept with her gold medal in her bed in the athletes' village. She pinched it when she woke up.

"Just to be sure it wasn't a dream," she said, "and that it's still going on. These are the best days of my life."

On a Roll

*T*ara began skating when she was only three years old. But her first pair of skates didn't have blades. Tara began skating with roller skates. By the time she was five, she had won regional roller-skating contests. Even after she tried ice skating, Tara continued to roller-skate. She was a national junior roller-skating champion at age nine.

When she was six, Tara decided to try skating on ice. She practiced at a rink in Delaware, near her home in Sewell, New Jersey. She didn't look like a champion skater the first time she tried on ice skates. "She was flopping around all over the place," her father recalled.

But with a few hours of practice, Tara transferred all she knew about roller-skating to figure skating. Soon she was doing the jumps and turns on ice skates that she had done on roller skates.

When Tara was nine, her family moved to Sugar Land, Texas. Tara's father, Jack, was an oil company executive and his job took him there. Tara soon found a place to skate. But it wasn't a typical skating rink. It was a rink in a shopping mall!

Tara would get up at three in the morning so she could practice figure skating at the rink in the Houston Galleria before school. After school she'd go back to the rink to practice some more.

At the rink it was easy to see Tara was something special every time she jumped. She pressed her lips together to concentrate on how her arms moved. She would work on making her turns smooth. And then she would effortlessly leave the ice, soaring into the air.

Tara worked long hours on her skating when she was younger.

At Home on the Ice

*T*ara missed her old skating rink in Delaware. One summer, two years after the family moved to Texas, Tara and her mother went back East so Tara could train at her old rink.

It went so well that Tara and her mother decided to stay. For two years, Tara and her mom lived in New Jersey while her dad lived in Texas.

It made a difference in Tara's skating career. In 1994, Tara took first place at the Olympic Sports Festival. She was 12 years, one month old, and was the youngest person to win a medal at the festival.

She had set high goals. "I want to go to the Olympics and win," she said after the festival.

At the 1995 U.S. Figure Skating Championships, Tara won the silver in the junior women's division. She finished fourth at the World Junior Championships.

Tara's skating was going well, but it was hard for Tara and her mom to be away from Tara's dad. The family kept in touch with daily phone calls.

"My parents are making a lot of sacrifices for me," Tara said. "Living away from my dad is hard because I can't see him every night. I miss him. It's especially hard on my mom. It has brought my mom and me closer, though."

"I'm not saying it's the greatest situation," Tara's mom said. "But we try to find ways to make it work."

Tara Lipinski at the World Championships.

A Move to Motown

In 1995, Tara and her mom moved again, this time to Michigan. Tara began training with a new coach, Richard Callaghan, at the Detroit Skating Club.

When her new coach saw her skate with U.S. men's champion Todd Eldredge, he realized he'd have to channel her spunky spirit. "Tara's attitude with Todd was, 'Whatever you can do, I can do better,' " Callaghan said.

The next year, Tara placed fifth at the world juniors. At the nationals, she competed as an adult and placed third. In women's world competition, she landed seven triple jumps in the long program and moved up from 23rd place to 15th.

Tara worked hard on her skating. She got up at 7:30 a.m. and got to the Detroit Skating Club after having breakfast with her mom. She practiced for 4 1/2 hours, taking a break after each 45-minute session on the ice.

Tara practicing in 1995.

Tara was determined to be perfect. Sometimes she wanted to practice a jump so many times that her coach had to ask her to please stop practicing!

Each afternoon tutors came to the condo Tara shared with her mom. She would study with them for four hours and do two hours of homework each night. Math and biology are her favorite courses. Some day she would like to go to college and become a lawyer.

For fun, Tara likes being with her friends, shopping, and going to the mall or movies. She has other hobbies, too, like ballet, jazz dance, gymnastics, tennis, and horseback riding.

"I like to relax on Sundays and watch TV," Tara said. "I like really old movies—the black-and-white ones, like those with Shirley Temple."

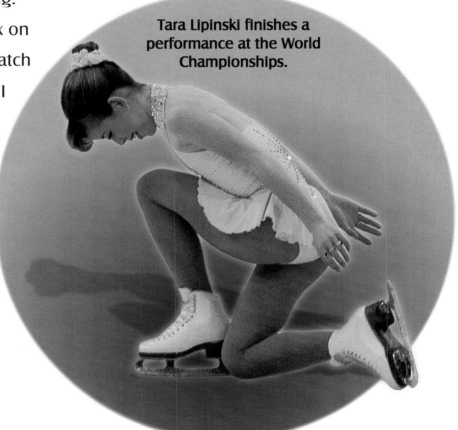

Tara Lipinski finishes a performance at the World Championships.

Best in the U.S.A.

*T*ara's difficult schedule paid off. In 1997, she traveled to Nashville, Tennessee, for the U.S. Figure Skating Championships.

"I just try to skate cleanly," she said, "and leave the rest up to the judges."

Michelle Kwan, the 1996 world champion, was favored to win the nationals. But Michelle fell twice during the long program.

Tara knew she had a chance.

"I was the next one on, so I had to retie my skates and get ready to go," Tara said. "I didn't have time to think, 'Oh, she didn't skate well; I have to win.' I just had to be confident and pretend it was a practice."

The 74-pound (33.5 kg) Tara was a tiny bundle of energy on the ice. She lifted her 4-foot, 9-inch (1.4 m) frame effortlessly, nailing difficult jumps. She awed the judges and audience. She became the youngest gold medalist in U.S. history!

"Winning was a surprise," she said afterward. "At first I was in shock, and for the rest of the night I acted all normal, but when I woke up the next day I was like, 'Oh my gosh! I can't believe it!' "

Left to right; Gusmeroli, Lipinski, and Kwan at the
1997 World Championships.

Visions of Gold

*A*fter she won the world competition, Tara had some fun. For nine days she visited her favorite place—Disney World! She has been there 14 times, once riding Splash Mountain all day long!

But even at Disney World she didn't forget about practicing her skating. She was going to practice for only half an hour, but she was concentrating so hard that soon two hours had gone by.

"Disney World is her favorite place, and she didn't care about it until she was satisfied with her skating," one of Tara's friends said. "She just loves it so much."

Tara with friend Erin Elbe on the Mad Tea Party attraction at Walt Disney World.

That year Tara also performed with other top skaters in the Campbell's Soups Tour of World Figure Skating Champions. In the midst of her busy schedule, Tara got to spend a weekend at home in Sugar Land.

"I played with my dogs, talked with my dad, watched TV, went to bed, and got up the next day and went swimming," Tara said. "I also went to see a movie. The whole day was really, really cool. I got to act normal."

Tara slept in her own room, where she has a poster of champions Jill Trenary, Katarina Witt, and Kurt Browning.

Tara with her dog, Coco.

"It's so strange," said Tara. "People say, 'So many kids look up to you,' but I'm still looking up to those top skaters."

Tara let herself daydream about winning the Olympic gold medal. "That would be pretty neat, you know?" she said. "Oh, OK, that would be really, really neat."

Stumble at Nationals

*I*n January 1998 Tara went to Philadelphia to compete in the U.S. Figure Skating Championships. She skated to music from the film *The Rainbow*.

"It's about a young girl growing up and facing fears and learning how to deal with things and just really loving what she does," Tara said. "For me, that's my skating."

Tara began the competition a little shaky. She stumbled on a triple flip in the short program. But instead of folding, she rallied. She pulled herself together and skated well the rest of the way.

However, Michelle Kwan had the performance of a lifetime. "In my mind, I was flying so high," Michelle said. "I was really having fun."

Tara finished second to Michelle at nationals, and then got ready for the Olympics.

Tara stumbles during her short program at the U.S. Figure Skating Championships (left). A good recovery the next day grabs her second place (below).

Good as Gold

*T*ara was excited to be competing at the Olympics, but she also made sure she enjoyed the experience. She marched in the opening ceremonies, and posed with 516-pound (234 kg) sumo wrestler Akebono. She got hockey star Wayne Gretzky's autograph. She answered e-mail at the press center.

"If I don't get an Olympic medal, what am I left with?" she said. "I want my Olympic memories. This is my chance to have fun."

She stayed in the athletes' village, rooming with 15-year-old ice dancer Jessica Joseph. "The Olympic Village energized me," she said. "And it relaxed me and made me not think about skating so much."

Callaghan knew Tara could handle staying on her own. "I knew she was organized enough to go to bed on time, get up on time, and not miss the bus to practice," he said. "Tara has her day structured so she's a giddy teenager between these hours and a really hard worker between these hours."

Tara knew she was ready, but she was the underdog to Michelle. "My biggest challenge was getting everyone to believe I had a chance," Tara said.

Tara studied tapes of her practices and got some hints from her choreographer on how to improve.

"I was looking at my presentation," Tara said, "and seeing myself on tape gave me confidence. Sometimes you think it's worse than it actually is."

Soon it was time to go to the White Ring for the short program. Tara skated to a song from the movie *Anastasia*. Dressed in a blue and yellow outfit, with a huge smile on her face, she did a triple flip, and skated fast and joyfully.

"I could actually see myself as Anastasia," Tara later said. "Emotionally, it was my best program ever."

Tara took second in the short program to Michelle, who excelled with a smooth, elegant style. Tara wasn't disappointed, though. "After the short program I was in a good spot," Tara said. "I always like to be the underdog and be very motivated."

Tara performing her short program at the 1998 Olympics.

In the long program, Michelle was solid but unspectacular. She left a tiny bit of room for someone to do better.

Right before the long program, Tara's coach told her, "I'm proud of you, you had a great two weeks here. You trained hard and had fun. Just go out and finish the experience."

Dressed in blue sequins, Tara performed the hardest free skate of anyone in the women's final. She skated with energy and passion. Her enthusiastic performance was almost perfect.

"I didn't breathe or feel a heartbeat for the four minutes she was skating," her father said.

Tara awed the audience with her trademark triple loop-triple loop combination, and her stunning final jump combination. "She was bursting with joy and relief," said Callaghan. "She looked excited to be out there."

Tara ran off the ice with her arms in the air. "I was thinking, 'Oh my gosh, I'm skating so well,' " Tara said. "I skated two great programs."

"Technically it was one of the greatest performances ever," CBS skating analyst Scott Hamilton said of the performance. "Tara had the difficulty and beautiful choreography as well."

"She had a totally different energy level from Michelle," added Eldredge. "Michelle skated not to lose, Tara skated to win."

As each score was posted, Tara let out an ear-piercing scream as she realized she had won the gold medal!

"I was so excited," Tara explained.

Tara beamed as she took her place on the medal podium, just as she had imagined herself doing when she was a toddler.

"It went by so quickly, it was sad to know I had to get off the medal stand," Tara said. "It was so wonderful, I couldn't think of anything wrong, anything negative. It felt so good and so perfect.

"I'm so happy. Anything from now on, I'll be able to do it." Tara held the medal in both hands after it was placed around her neck.

"I wasn't thinking about winning or about beating anyone," Tara said. "I just went out and told myself that I didn't want to be disappointed when I left the ice. I felt like this was one of the best programs I've ever done. I was at the Olympics, I was skating great and that showed through."

Tara celebrates after completing her free skate program.

Going Pro

*A*fter the Olympics, Tara savored her gold medal.

"I'm just going to walk around enjoying being an Olympic champion," she said.

But the experience tired her out. She went home to Sugar Land to rest and spend time with her family.

"I had a little heart-to-heart with her," her father said. "This living apart (while Tara trained) has been hard on us as a family. We see each other on weekends, but it's tough. And when she came back to Houston (for the victory parade), you could just see her eyes light up.

Tara with her parents, Jack and Patricia Lipinski.

She was back in her room, with her dogs and her friends. She was home."

In April 1998, Tara announced she would turn pro. She wanted to spend more time with her family.

"Now I'll have four-day weekends and be able to be with my family. I don't want to be 21 years old and not know my dad," Tara said. "I realized after Nagano how important it is to me to be with my mom and dad.

Tara making her professional debut on Friday, April 24, 1998.

"I've accomplished my dream. I think I need to give something back to them, so we can be a family again and really have that connection."

But Tara's fans don't have to worry. She'll still be skating in front of cheering audiences, performing her spins and jumps with the bubbly enthusiasm that helped her reach the top.

Tara's Profile

Height: 4' 10"

Weight: 82 pounds

Birth date: June 10, 1982

Parents: Jack and Pat Lipinski

Resides in: Sugar Land, Texas

Coaches: Richard Callaghan and

Megan Faulkner

Tara has her own Web site:

www.taralipinski.com

Chronology

1982 - Born in Philadelphia on June 10

1991 - Family moves from Sewell, New Jersey, to Sugar Land, Texas

1993 - Tara and her mother, Pat, return to New Jersey so Tara can train at her old ice rink

1994 - Tara places first at U.S. Olympic Festival
   She also places:
   Second at National Novice
   First at Southwestern Novice
   First at Midwestern Novice
   First at Blue Swords

1995 - Tara wins silver medal at U.S. Junior Championships
   Takes fourth place at World Junior Championships
   Tara and her mother move to Detroit so Tara can train with
   coach Richard Callaghan

1996 - Tara places third at U.S. Figure Skating Championships

She also places:

15th at World Championships

Fifth at World Junior Championships

Second at World Junior Selections Competition

First at South Atlantic Juniors

Second at Skate Canada

Third at Trophy Lalique

Second at Nations Cup

1997 - Tara wins first place at the World Championships

She also places:

First at U.S. Figure Skating Championships

First at Championship Series

First at Hershey's Challenge (team)

Second at Skate America

Second at Trophy Lalique

1998 - Tara takes second at National Championships

Places first in the Champion Series Final

Wins gold medal at the Olympic Games in Nagano, Japan

In April announces her decision to turn pro

Tara's top finishes

1994

First at U.S. Olympic Festival

Second at National Novice

First at Southwestern Novice

First at Midwestern Novice

First at Blue Swords

Tara gets excited when she learns she has won the gold medal.

1995

Fourth at World Junior Championships

Second at U.S. Figure Skating Junior Championships

Fourth at Nebelhorn Trophy

1996

Third at U.S. Figure Skating Championships

15th at World Championships

Fifth at World Junior Championships

Second at World Juniors Selections Competition

First at South Atlantic Juniors

Second at Skate Canada

Third at Trophy Lalique

Second at Nations Cup

1997

First at World Championships

First at U.S. Figure Skating Championships

First in Championship Series Final

First at Hershey's Challenge (team)

Second at Skate America

Second at Trophy Lalique

1998

First at Winter Olympic
    Games

Second at U.S. Figure
    Skating Championships

First at Champion
    Series Final

Glossary

FLIP - A jump performed by pushing off with the teeth on the front of the skate blades. The skater spins in the air and lands on the opposite foot.

GOLD MEDAL - Prize given to the winner of certain competitions.

JUNIOR - Competition for younger athletes.

LONG PROGRAM - Free skating portion of figure skating competition, set to music, usually four minutes long for women. No specific moves are required.

LOOP - A jump performed by taking off on the back outside edge of a skate, turning in the air, and landing on the same edge.

NATIONALS - The U.S. Figure Skating Championships.

OLYMPICS - International athletic contest held every two years, alternating between summer and winter events.

REGIONAL - An event involving competitors from a particular area.

RINK - An enclosed expanse of ice used for skating.

SHORT PROGRAM - A two-minute, 40-second performance in figure skating, set to music, requiring eight elements.

TRIPLE LOOP - A loop jump with three revolutions.

WORLDS - The World Figure Skating Championships.

Index